SKAR
BR

the late **V Go**
formerly Professor of Archaeology a.   ͟institute of
Archaeology in the Univer.   ͟n

D V Clarke
National Museum of Antiquities of Scotland, Edinburgh

Edinburgh
Her Majesty's Stationery Office

The Site Revealed

In the winter of 1850 a storm of exceptional severity stripped the grass from the high dune known as Skara Brae (or Skeroo Brae) in the south corner of the Bay of Skaill and an immense midden or refuse heap and the ruins of ancient dwellings were thereby exposed to view. The laird of Skaill, William Watt, began to explore the site and by 1868, four of the houses described below had been cleared out and a very rich collection of objects had been deposited in Skaill House. The site was then left undisturbed, apart from some casual digging in 1913, until the end of 1925. In December of that year another terrific storm washed away part of the midden and damaged parts of the previously cleared structures. The ruins had by then been

placed under the guardianship of the Commissioners of HM Office of Works by W G T Watt's trustees. To prevent further storm damage, the Commissioners first had the present sea-wall built to secure the foundations of the site and subsequently undertook the consolidation of the buildings. The latter work, carried out from 1927 to 1930, involved the clearing out of new dwellings and some soundings below the level of the existing walls and floors. The archaeological aspects of this exercise were supervised by the late Professor Childe. In 1972 and 1973 further excavation took place in order to collect samples for radiocarbon determinations, a form of dating independant of archaeological techniques and not available at the time of Childe's work, and to recover further information

concerning the environment during the site's occupation and the economic basis of the lives of the inhabitants. Analysis of the finds from this recent work is still going on but some preliminary conclusions have been incorporated in the information given below.

Excavations in 1972 and 1973 were carried out in the centre of the site, revealing evidence for earlier houses.

Professor Childe examines a section during his excavations.

House 1 as revealed by the storm of 1850.

The Best in Northern Europe

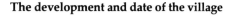

The development and date of the village

Skara Brae is the best preserved prehistoric village in northern Europe, but its importance lies not only in the height of the surviving walls but also in the presence of major items of furniture in each house. It is one of the very few sites where the construction of a picture of the interior of a prehistoric house is not a wholly imaginative exercise. This is principally because the furniture, like the houses, was constructed from local flagstone, the bedding-planes of which make it possible for large flat slabs which do not require dressing to be easily quarried. Considerable areas of flagstone can be seen exposed on the beach close to the site.

The remains which we can see today consist of a cluster of six self-contained houses and a workshop, connected by covered passages or alleys. The houses are buried to the tops of the surviving walls in a huge heap of midden consisting of ash, shells, broken bones and similar refuse, mixed with sand and possessing in some instances the consistency of clay. The same midden lay upon the slabs that roof the passages between the dwellings. Indeed, this protective cocoon of midden has been a major element in ensuring the remarkable preservation of the site. Similar objects were found in the midden and on the floor of the houses, whose walls are not founded on rock nor on natural sand but on the levelled remains of houses and middens resulting from previous human occupation. This occupation must plainly precede the erection of the houses upon its debris and parts of several houses from this earlier period may still be seen. Our knowledge of this initial period of settlement is rather fragmentary since its remains can only be explored in areas which do not have later buildings on top of them. The results of the recent excavations have suggested that there were two main periods of occupation although the

The bay of Skaill today: when the village was occupied this may have been a fresh-water lagoon.

5

site does not seem to have been abandoned between these two periods and many aspects of life were the same throughout the existence of the settlement. What did change, however, was the overall plan of the village and, to a lesser extent, the design of the houses. Although there is some coincidence in the siting of houses (house 4, for instance, largely overlies the remains of an earlier house, 4'), it is now clear that the structures in the earlier period 1 were located in different places from the houses of the later period 2. In other words, the period 2 houses which are the best preserved today do not represent a rebuilding of earlier houses on the same site. A change in the design of the houses accompanied this alteration in overall layout so that the beds which had been recessed into the thickness of the house-walls in period 1 were constructed as free-standing units projecting from the walls in period 2. Both periods 1 and 2 saw a considerable amount of small-scale repair and alteration but this did not radically alter the general plan of the village.

Before the excavations in 1972 and 1973, the only means of dating the site was comparison of the finds with dated material in the south of England. Inevitably, the wide geographical separation of the two groups led to various interpretations of the date of Skara Brae. It is now clear from radiocarbon determinations that occupation of the site began a little before 3100 BC and ended around 2500 BC. Within these six hundred years the two main periods in the settlement's history were of almost equal duration although it seems that period 2 may have been marginally longer than period 1.

The first settlers at Skara Brae seem to have camped on a sloping plain some 6m above sea-level. The sea would not, however, have been as close to the site as it is today and it is possible that the site was adjacent to a freshwater lagoon in an area where water was ponded up behind the foredunes. The Bay of Skaill would certainly have been very much smaller and the shoreline some distance away to the west. Despite these differences in the coastal areas there would have been considerable similarities between the environment then and now. Although a birch and hazel scrub with a rich understorey of herbs and ferns had once existed on Mainland, by the time the first inhabitants arrived at Skara Brae most of that cover had already disappeared, possibly as a result of a regional increase in wind-speed. During the time the village was occupied pasture was established and consolidated so that the general appearance of the land and its vegetation would have been similar to that of today. The one major difference would have been the absence of large areas of peat, much of which did not form until well after the abandonment of Skara Brae.

The reasons for the evacuation of the village are far from clear. Childe believed that it was the result of a major storm similar to the one which first exposed the site in 1850. However, the evidence in support of this view is far from conclusive and it is unlikely that we will ever be able to offer a definitive answer. What is clear is that the village does not seem to have been attacked, since no sign of fighting or looting was recorded during any of the excavations. After the main occupation had ceased, groups of people squatted in the half-buried houses – traces of the hearths and refuse associated with them were found in house 7. No firm indication of the date of this use of the site is available. Finally, when the village had been entirely buried in sand, an old man and a young woman were interred in rough coffins formed of stone slabs set into pits dug in the sand. There were no grave-goods by which they might be dated but the manner of burial suggests they might be of the early centuries AD, perhaps even Norse. Certainly, these burials mark the end of human occupation at Skara Brae.

The Village and its Inhabitants

The general character of the ruins

The ruins now conserved consist of a cluster of houses with the main items of furniture in each. Before describing the actual remains, it is convenient to summarise certain general features common to most of the structures.

The walls are built for the most part of flagstone blocks, easily quarried and readily available from the large areas exposed on the beach. Freestone slabs brought from farther afield are occasionally to be seen. A finely-bedded shale resembling slate was often used for the roofs of passages and for pavements. The walls are all of dry-stone masonry, built without the use of mortar. The stonework, however, often provides only an inner and outer facing for a central core of clay and midden. Whether the interstices were plugged with clay is uncertain but there is some evidence to suggest that the outer faces were plastered with clay when they projected beyond the surrounding midden.

The houses are roughly rectangular in plan, but the corners are always internally rounded. In size the houses vary from 6.4m by 6.1m to 4.3m by 4m. The walls, standing in one case over 2.4m high, tend to corbel inwards with each course projecting slightly beyond the one below. This is most notable in the corners. It is practically certain that this corbelling was never built high enough to cover the whole house with a beehive roof. Instead, the roof is likely to have been of turf

House 1.

or skins resting on wooden or whalebone rafters, although we have very little evidence on this point. The walls, which are often over 1m thick, would have provided an ample platform for the secure bedding of the rafters. As stated above, a large part of the walls was surrounded outside with refuse. This refuse, however, did not pile up around the pre-existing houses and is not, in large measure, the product of their inhabitants. Instead, the structures were set in hollows cut into previously accumulated midden heaps, presumably to effect the maximum weatherproofing.

Each of the houses was entered by a single doorway piercing the thick walls and in no case more than 1.2m high. The entrance is constricted by a pair of jambs and a threshold stone so that the average size at this point is only 1.1m high by 0.6m wide. Immediately inside the jambs may be seen, in the side walls, holes designed to hold the bar that fastened the door proper, possibly a stone slab.

In the centre of every house is a square fireplace formed by four stone kerbs. Against the walls on either side of the hearth may be

The entrance to house 7.

seen beds made of stone slabs set on edge. That on the right of the entrance is always the larger, the dimensions ranging from 2m by 1m to 1.5m by 0.8m. Similar fixed beds, only formed of wooden planks, were still in use in some parts of Norway earlier this century. In front of the beds at either end may be seen the stumps of tall slabs set on end like pillars. They probably supported some sort of canopy over the beds, like those described by Dr Mitchell as being used last century to shelter the beds in the Hebridean blackhouses. We must remember that we have here only the basic framework of the beds. They would probably have been lined with plants such as bracken or heather, and there would have been coverings of sheep or other animal skins.

The hearth in house 7.

A bed in house 7.

9

Immediately above the beds, one or two recesses in the walls are generally to be seen. These presumably acted as open cupboards. Enclosures similar to the beds are often found against the front wall to the left of the door and in one of the corners. The former may well also have served as beds but those in the corners were generally paved with slates at a level above the house floor and probably acted as storage areas. Against the wall opposite the door in every house there is a stone cupboard, generally two-storied, and supported by three legs in the front. It appears to have fulfilled the same function as a modern dresser: there is no reason to believe it was an altar, as some have suggested.

Let into the floor in one corner of every house are three or more small boxes formed of thin slabs. The joints have always been found to be carefully luted with clay as if to make them water-tight but nothing has been discovered which reveals their use. They may perhaps have been used to soak limpets, which seem to have been a prime source of fish-bait. Limpets require soaking in fresh water to soften the hard outer edge in order to make them more attractive to the fish. By having a number of boxes and using them in rotation it would be possible to have freshly prepared bait available all the time.

A cupboard in house 7.

The dresser in house 7.

Two boxes in house 1.

One or more cells set in the thickness of the walls open off each house. Some are beehive-shaped, about 1.2m in diameter and as high at their tallest point. Others are like little blind passages with flat roofs. In some cells collections of fine bone beads and elaborately worked implements were discovered, suggesting that these served as treasure chambers. In some houses, the end of the hole into which the bar securing the door was manoeuvred opens into a cell which may thus be interpreted as a sort of guard-room. On the other hand drains – shallow, stone-lined channels roofed with flagstones – lead away from the floor of at least three cells, which are best interpreted as latrines.

The entrance to cell 4 in house 1.

The interior of cell 4 in house 1.

The main passage.

The midden heap, which surrounds the houses, is itself an integral part of the building materials used by the inhabitants. Just how it was used is unclear, but its presence around all the houses is not the result of the haphazard disposal of rubbish. The recent excavations showed that the mound of midden was already in position when the passages were built, by in effect, cutting a channel in the midden and lining it with dry-stone masonry. It seems likely that the houses were similarly inserted into a pre-existing midden heap. The purpose of this unusual arrangement of largely subterranean houses linked by passages was evidently to secure really efficient shelter from the winds and storms so prevalent in these northerly latitudes.

The passages link all the houses together so that it would not have been necessary to go outside to move between them. These narrow passages were generally about 1.2m high and roofed with stone lintels. Along their length were doorways and bar-holes exactly comparable to those of the individual houses but they eventually led out on to paved areas open to the sky beyond the midden heap. The site, indeed, must

originally have appeared as a low, rounded mound. From its surface the roofs of the houses would have been the only breaks in its sides.

The inhabitants of the village were essentially pastoralists, in the sense that they depended heavily on the products of their herds of cattle and flocks of sheep. To judge from the bones incorporated in the midden these two species formed the staple food, but their diet was diversified by a number of other items. Fishing was particularly important to judge from the number of bones recovered in the recent excavations, with limpets being collected primarily as bait rather than for human consumption. Variety was also provided by small amounts of crab and other shellfish, pig, venison, birds' eggs and possibly even the birds themselves. The role of plants is much less easy to determine, although much work still remains to be done in this field on the evidence recovered in the recent excavations. We have, however, good reason to suppose that plants form an important part of the food-supply in economies like that of Skara Brae, although their perishable nature make this point difficult to demonstrate. Some grain, mainly

Modern examples of the sea food caught by the inhabitants.

Bone tools and a piece of haematite (bottom right), probably used in preparing skins.

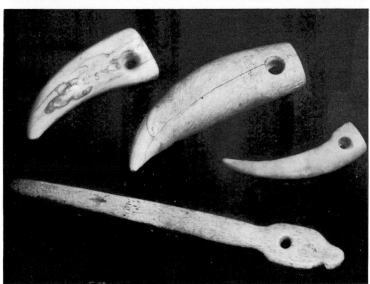

Bone pin and pendants.

15

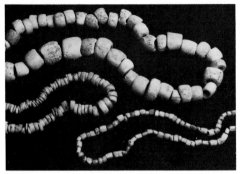

Beads.

Pottery.

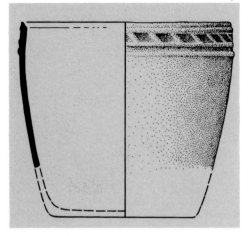

Stone and bone containers for red ochre – a substance from which red paint can be made.

Part of a wooden handle, possibly for an axe.

Recent drift wood drying against the wall of the mill at Skaill.

barley, was recovered from the earliest midden and other deposits yielded hazel nut shells.

For clothing the villagers probably relied upon the skins of various animals. Many of the bone-tools found at the site seem best adapted for use in preparing skins whereas textile-manufacturing appliances are absent. Individual jewellery took the form of bone and ivory pins (often with elaborate heads), pendants and beads. The latter in particular are made from a wide variety of material including animal, bird and fish bones, shell, killer-whale teeth, walrus or narwhal ivory, and stone. Small stone cups and limpet-shells retaining traces of red ochre suggest perhaps body painting, although a desire to colour the stones, particularly the decorated examples, is equally likely.

Pottery was manufactured in some quantity, although the quality is often poor. The range of sizes is considerable, from small thumb-pots to large storage jars some 60cm in diameter. Much of it is decorated, usually with applied strips forming simple geometric patterns. The bone tools are numerous, both in terms of quantity and the range of types, and they seem to have formed the main tool-kit for the inhabitants, although wood may also have been an important component. The recent excavations recovered fragments of several wooden tools, even though wood only survives in one midden deposit which happened to be waterlogged. As we noted above, usable timber would not have been growing locally, but large quantities are likely to have been deposited on the beaches as driftwood from North America. Several pieces have already been identified as spruce, which can only have come from that source. Another material deposited as drift, this time from Iceland, was pumice, which was used as an abrasive in the manufacture of bone and wooden tools. Much of the stonework is of poor quality, but this reflects the lack of suitable raw material, such as large nodules of flint, rather than the absence of

skill among the inhabitants, for some of the spiked balls, presumably for ritual use, show the incredible dexterity and skill of their makers.

The community seems to have been largely self-sufficient. Certainly, there is nothing among the finds that could not have been made from material available in Orkney, although obtaining some things, for example haematite from the north coast of Hoy, may well have involved contact with other villages. Coined money was, of course, unknown.

Stone axes.

Carved stone objects, presumably for ritual use.

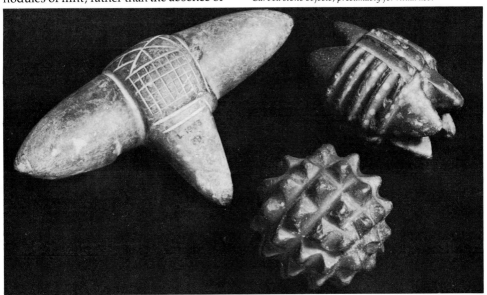

17

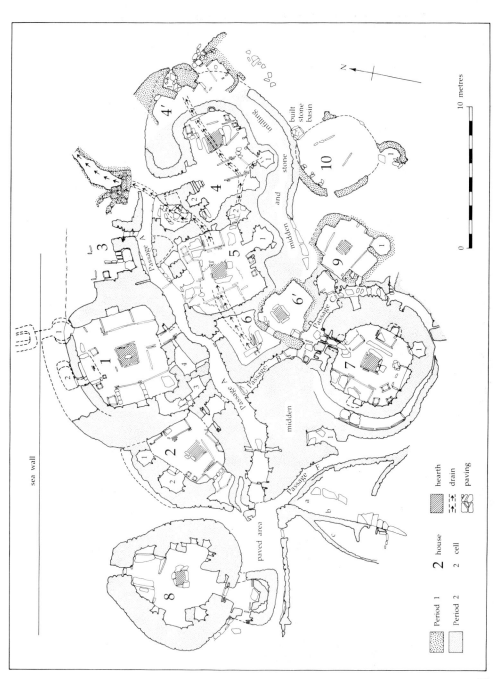

A Guided Tour

The Ruins
Period 2 (The Later Period)

On entering the enclosure the visitor has on his left the outer wall of the easternmost house in the village, **house 4** on the plan. On the east a section of the original outer face of the house wall is still exposed, running across the ruins of an earlier structure, no. 4'. The bottom course of this wall is formed of massive blocks on edge with small stones fitted very neatly into the corners. It was coated with a layer of blue clay, 23 cm thick, to keep out the damp. A midden platform some 2.7m wide surrounded this house and the adjacent house, no. 5. Portions of the retaining wall supporting this platform are still visible.

At its foot are the fragmentary remains of a slab pavement. This paved area marks the east end of passage A, the main artery of the village, and forms a convenient guide to a perambulation of the ruins. Passage A is closed to visitors who must use the steps on its seaward side.

The first opening on the left is the passage 3.7m long, leading into house 4. It is narrowed by the door-jambs of the house, and just on the house side of the jambs the bar-hole is visible: a stone bar for securing the door was found in position in the hole. The bar-hole runs through into a beehive cell, opening on to the interior of the house to the right of the door. A carved stone ball was found in the cell in 1928. There is a second beehive cell, very perfectly preserved, in the rear wall just opposite the doorway. A shallow drain, covered with slabs (no longer visible), leads from this cell under the house floor to join a second that runs from house 5 eastwards across house 4. The pillars of the dresser may be seen to the left of the cell entrance. House 4 was built up against the east wall of house 5.

Returning to the main passage, A, one sees, still on the left, a turfed-over entrance-cell floor in the bastion between houses 4 and 5 with a stone mortar in it. The floor of this little chamber, 38 cm above the pavement of the passage, is itself the roof of a tiny cell (no longer visible) entered from house 5. Just in front of house 3, between the sea walk and the beginning of passage A, is a hatch. This gives access to a sewer 30 m to 51 cm deep and 41 cm to 102 cm wide roofed with lintel-slabs 114 cm below the pavement of passage A. The sewer which runs under the passage in one direction and seaward in the other, was probably constructed before period 2.

A little further on, on the right, is the doorway to **house 3** (between passage A and the foot of the modern steps). The northern and eastern walls had already been washed away last century, and the storm of 1925 demolished other pieces of furniture – the uprights of a dresser and several tanks – shown in earlier plans. The walls of a small cell on the left of the door can still be made out, together with part of the main room of the house.

Passage A begins to descend gently from the entrance to house 4. Just beyond house 3 a triangular cell, 1.8 m wide by 1.4 m deep, will be noticed on the left. The slabs over the entrance are supported by a central pillar. Immediately beyond it is a sort of bench over looked by a window from house 5. At about this spot Mr Watt found an incomplete human skeleton. The passage is here traversed by a slab on edge forming a step down. It may mark the site of a gate, of which the upright slab would be the sole surviving jamb.

House 5 is entered immediately beyond this point. The doorway has been destroyed by earlier excavators but is shown complete in a plan published in *The Proceedings of the Society of Antiquaries of Scotland*, 1868. The house is otherwise well preserved, notably the central fireplace (now filled with brown quarry dust), the beds on either side, the pillars of the dresser against the rear wall and the tanks in the corners and under the dresser. A beehive cell in the rear wall was entered from below the latter. A very ruinous cell in the left-hand rear corner is paved with slate and is served by the drain already mentioned as running across the floor of house 4. A square slab of freestone in the wall behind the left-hand bed blocks the entry to a very narrow passage, never more than 76 cm high and in places only 25 cm wide, that leads eventually to the cell, previously mentioned, in the bastion between houses 4 and 5. The cell was about 91 cm square and contained a large stone mortar (now lying on the turf above) and two whales' vertebrae. A peculiarity of house 5 is the window piercing the front wall to the left of the door and looking on to passage A. It is the only instance of a window in the village, and may indicate that passage A was never roofed east of the supposed gate mentioned above.

House 1 opens on the right of passage A, a metre or so beyond the door to house 5. The entrance is perfectly preserved, the walls being faced with slabs perforated for the bar-hole, which is controlled from a cell on the left. The rear wall of the house, including the window, was reconstructed on the seaward side by Mr Watt in the nineteenth century;

there is no evidence that the window was an original feature. There were certainly two cells in the house, one in the right-hand corner, served by a drain, and the other behind the dresser. The latter is original and the remaining fittings are well-preserved. Note particularly the 'bedposts' on the left, which were probably taller to support a canopy, and the paved enclosures in the two southern corners. A stone axe-head was found by Mr Watt in the keeping-place above the right-hand bed, while the large stone basin, or mortar, now to the right of the dresser, lay near the hearth. Two cells survive: one, opening just on the left of the doorway, commands the bar-hole of the door and a spy-hole looking out on to the main passage. A low door in the left-hand fore corner of the house gives access to a narrow passage running between the walls of houses 1 and 2 and leading to a small cell, 1.2 m square and 1 m high, between the front wall and passage A. At one time this cell was entered from passage A, and the doorway, roughly blocked up in antiquity, is still discernible. A hoard of 2,400 beads, several pendants and pins, and a whalebone dish filled with red pigment, were discovered in this cell in 1928. It should be noted that both houses 2 and 3 are later than house 1, having been built on to it, but the difference in time may have been short.

In places passage A is still roofed with the original lintel slabs beyond the door to house 1. Originally the slabs were covered by a layer of midden, 30 cm or more deep, that ran right up to the edges of houses 5, 3, 1 and 2. The same midden heap originally stretched continuously over the area now occupied by the turfed area south of passage A, right to house 7.

A doorway on the left of passage A now gives access to this area. It may have been designed as the entrance to **house 6** built against the outer wall of house 5. Even though part of the retaining wall of house 5 was demolished, it would still have been a very small house in comparison with the others in the village. In the event it seems never to have been completed, and the door led only to a cell the walls of which were too ruinous to conserve.

House 2 is eventually reached on the right of passage A, the door proper being entered through a tiny antechamber or 'hall'. This house is the smallest in the village and is built on to house 1. The rear, seaward wall has been badly ruined, but the walls of two cells are still distinguishable in it, as well as the supports of a dresser in front of the left-hand cell. Just behind the central hearth was the stump of a stone slab on end that once stood 46 cm high but has now decayed. Bone mattock-heads and unfinished beads were found on the floor between the hearth and the beds. The surviving bed-post of the right-hand bed is nearly perfect, but the posts for the left-hand bed are absent, the end-slabs of the beds being made specially tall in compensation. There is an inexplicable pillar on the left of the door and a keeping-place above the now sloping door-lintel.

Opposite the entrance to house 2, a side passage, B on plan, joins the main passage. Its floor is now 51 cm below the pavement of passage A. A huge accumulation of limpet shells was found filling passage B up to the level of passage A when it was cleared in 1928. Passage B leads downward under the midden, its floor at its farther end being about 61 cm lower than at its junction with A. The passage of course originally ran under a midden heap about a metre deep. It was probably interrupted by a gate 4 m from its mouth and seems to terminate in a sort of cell behind the inner wall of house 7.

Just in front of the mouth of this cell passage B is joined on the left by a third passage, termed C. The latter was originally roofed-over and buried in midden, but in the first 3.7 m the roofing slabs had collapsed in antiquity, allowing the superincumbent refuse to fall into the passage after the latter had filled with a mere 61 cm of drift sand.

House 7 opens on to this section of passage C. It is the most perfect dwelling in the village, and has been covered with a glass roof to ensure its continued preservation. The doorway, paved and faced with 'slate' slabs, resembles that of house 1, except that the end of the bar-hole is controlled from the cell opening on to passage B, not on to the interior of the hut. Nevertheless, the bar could still have been operated from inside the house. Immediately behind the fireplace is a cubical block of stone, perhaps a seat or working-surface. The long slab lying to the left of the hearth was probably originally a bed-post. In its fall it crushed a pot, fragments of which were found beneath it in 1928. On the right of the entrance is a low enclosed dais; on its pavement were found a large basin of whalebone, a stone mortar, and two cooking pots filled with animal bones. In the left-hand front corner a tiny whalebone dish, full of red pigment, stood embedded on the floor. Two stone mortars were set in the floor in the corresponding rear corner, while close beside them lay two bone mattock-heads and a shovel made from an ox's shoulder-blade. The beds, dresser, tanks and keeping-places are thoroughly typical, but the solid block of masonry on the left of the doorway and the numerous small rectangular holes (looking suspiciously suitable for joists) in the topmost courses of the walls deserve notice. The upper edge of the slab bounding the right-hand bed bears a series of deeply incised markings, worn away over most of its length but clearly visible where the slab was protected by the bed-posts. The markings have suggested an inscription to some but are more likely to be merely decorative.

The wall behind the bed is partially faced with a thin slab. The latter rests on a horizontal slab, projecting from beneath the wall flush with the floor of the bed. This slab covered a grave in which lay the skeletons of two old women buried in a crouched attitude on their sides. These bodies had evidently been deliberately interred here beneath the foundation of the hut wall. There is no reason to suppose that the women were sacrificed for the occasion, but the idea was doubtless that of intimately associating the structure with the ancestors of its inhabitants. This seems to have been a widespread practice, well-documented ethnologically. The cell in the back of the house to the east of the dresser is of the beehive type, 1.3m high, and was found to contain a small hoard of beads and pendants and a broken pot.

Passage C continues beyond the door of house 7 between the walls of that structure and older dwellings of period 1. The roofing slabs are missing until the north-east corner of house 7 is reached. There the passage is narrowed by an extra facing-wall, built on to the outside of house 7, to a width of only 56 cm. At this point a beehive cell, no longer visible, opens off on the left. The passage itself runs on with its original roof intact, curving round the outside of house 7. It slopes up gradually in so doing, till its pavement is 122 cm above the floor of house 7. At the corner there are indications of a gate. Just over two metres beyond the gate the roofing slabs come to an end, and a gap in the left-hand wall leads up and out on to the original surface of the midden heap. The passage itself runs on for 3.7 m and then stops short just behind the beehive cell in house 7. Beyond its end were found the remains of the intrusive stone cist or coffin which contained the body of a young woman. As already noted (p 6) this burial had nothing to do with the original occupation of the site and was laid down when the ruins were already buried in sand. On the opposite side of house 7 a sort of

gallery, 66 cm to 86 cm wide, and paved with slabs at a height of 147 cm above the house floor, ran partly round the structure and across the roof of the cell at the end of passage B. The function of this gallery is unknown. It might conceivably have continued as a second storey over passage C to the gap above the door to house 7. But it was actually found full of midden and may have been intended only as a sort of damp course. It has now been refilled and is no longer visible.

Returning to the main passage A, we have a section 4.3 m long over which the original roofing slabs had become so badly cracked before the passage was cleared that they had to be removed. It ends in a gate formed by two slabs projecting from the side walls to serve as jambs with a space only 53 cm wide between them. They support a freestone lintel 104 cm above a transverse projecting sill. Just inside, the jambs, to the east, are bar-holes. The bar slid in a specially built channel in the midden on the left.

Just over 2 m beyond the gate the passage is again constricted by a second pair of jambs, 53 cm apart, supporting a flagstone lintel 99 cm from the floor. Some of the stones (now covered by glass sheets) on the left-hand side of this outer gate bear scratched geometric designs, while a stone in the right-hand wall of the passage, just beyond the entry to house 2, shows markings formed by battering or 'picking' its surface. Beyond the outer gate the passage contracts once more and then gives out on to a paved area.

The decorated edge of a slab forming part of a bed in house 7.

The **Market Place**, as this has been nicknamed, was never roofed-over, and was found full of pure drift sand. Its floors consist of two layers of slabs resting on a blue clay bedding. A test-pit sunk here had to pass through 2.4 m of earlier deposits before reaching the natural subsoil.

On the right of the Market Place stands **structure 8**. Alone among all the buildings unearthed at Skara Brae, it stands entirely free of the midden. The outer wall, exposed all round to the elements, rests on heavy slabs set edgewise in the same blue-clay bedding as supports the Market Place pavement. This type of construction has been noted outside house 4. These slabs supported a platform of rubble masonry around the building proper.

The structure is anomalous in several respects. There are no tanks let into the floor, nor built beds. There are, however, wide alcoves on either side of the hearth corresponding in position and size to the normal beds. Instead of a dresser, there seems to have been a deep recess in the rear, seaward, wall, partitioned off from the main chamber by thin slabs set on edge. Within the apsidal area thus marked off is a rectangular paved space framed by two stout slabs standing on edge at right-angles to the other slabs. This area, now, like the main room of the structure, floored with quarry dust, was packed with volcanic stones fractured by heat. In the rear wall is a gap 38 cm wide interrupted only by a very low sill stone. An immense number of chert chips were found scattered over the whole floor. Both the internal layout and the finds suggest that this was not an ordinary dwelling, and it seems best interpreted as a specialised workshop for the making of chert tools. The volcanic stones would have been used in a process of controlled heating and cooling of the chert nodules in order to make them easier to flake.

The building is at present entered through a porch, built on to its southern end on the western side of the Market Place. There are traces of an earlier entrance just in front of the porch. The porch itself is very flimsily built. It was covered with a flat slate roof and had originally boasted a second entrance on the west, opposite to the present doorway that gives on to the Market Place. One jamb of the old west entrance is still visible from the outside, but the gap had been blocked up during the life of the structure and an additional corbelled lining built up inside the present outer wall. The workshop itself is entered from the porch by a doorway equipped with the usual bar-holes. Inside the door on the right is a secondary buttress, perhaps connected with the blocking of the original entrance. A number of stones in the wall bear finely engraved or scratched patterns. A design of hatched lozenges on a smooth stone to the right of the doorway (covered by a glass sheet) is one of the best attempts at a pattern in the village. A pillar of sandy flagstone that originally stood beside the hearth also bore rather obscure patterns formed by battering with a blunt implement.

The Market Place is bordered on the south by a rather flimsy retaining wall that seems to end abruptly, flush with the west side of structure 8. Between this wall and the house porch is a paved way that forms a sort of unroofed continuation of passage A. The pavement, however, stops short by the west door of the porch. The blue-clay bedding continued beyond this point for some distance, dipping steeply downwards, but no further traces of buildings have come to light. It is uncertain how much the deposits extend in this direction.

On reaching the Market Place from passage A, now turfed over, a paved way is seen leading out seaward between the walls of house 2 and structure 8. The end of the paving has been disturbed by the waves, but it seems merely to have led out on to the midden surface. On the left of the Market Place a corresponding paved way, termed passage F, leads in a south-easterly direction. This way may indeed once have been roofed over. The left-hand wall forms the south-eastern boundary of the central heap of

Nicknamed the
Market Place, this may
have been just a paved
area at the entrance to
the main passage.

Structure 8, probably
a workshop.

refuse. After a length of 6.4 m, this wall breaks off and here, to the east, there is a narrow cell originally roofed with horizontal slate slabs. One of the upright slabs of the cell bears incised marks and small round pits.

The right-hand wall of passage F, lettered 'a' on the plan, continues further than the paving though everywhere very ruinous so as to form, with the outside wall of house 7, a sort of passage descending along the surface of the old period 1 midden heap. There was no compact midden behind wall a but rather drift sand interrupted by thin layers of midden material. On the uppermost of these, deposited when passage F was already partly choked with sand, a slab-paved track leading out from the Market Place had been laid down, and is still partly visible as slabs laid on the turf. To make room for it a strip of wall a had been broken down so that it no longer joins on to the south wall of the Market Place. Two walls at present run from between the latter wall and the break in wall a. The better-preserved of these (lettered 'b') has been uncovered for a distance of 9.1 m and certainly continues still farther inland. In it were two gaps (one still visible) which gave access to very flimsy cell-like structures of stone, the southernmost of which can still be seen. The wall with its annexe rests on a layer of midden material about 15 cm thick. Under this is a layer of sand.

The midden layer (and at the corner, wall b itself) runs over the stumps of an older wall, c, that runs south-west. At its foot is a pavement of thick slabs, some of which are carved. This paving rests on the same blue-clay bedding as the Market Place and structure 8 – throughout the history of the site blue clay was used as a foundation material. Beneath this comes 2.13 m to 2.44 m of older refuse.

The function of all these flimsy walls is unknown. All seem to be built up against banked sand. Possibly, therefore, they were erected in the vain hope of checking the encroachment of sand dunes advancing from the south-west (the direction of the most prevalent wind). On the surface of the dunes, formed against each of these temporary checks, midden material may have been deliberately laid down as if to provide a capping for the less stable sand.

There are no indications of any important structures of period 2 beyond the limits of the existing excavations, and, except along the line of wall b, even the older midden deposits upon which the extant village stands are known to have been thinning out. The recent excavations have shown, however, that the deposits are still of considerable depth.

Period 1 (The Earlier Period)

As already noted, the present houses stand upon the refuse accumulated in an earlier period and even upon the ruins of older structures. Some of these have been laid bare and are still visible. On the removal of the great block of midden that once ran continuously across the roof of passage A right to the edge of the wall round house 7 one such structure, termed **house 6'** was exposed. It seems at one time to have opened on to what is now passage C, almost opposite the entry to house 7.

All that is now visible are the hearth and the stumps of the walls (a stone in the north wall bears an engraved pattern). The house floor was buried by a deposit of sand, 46 cm to 61 cm thick. Over this and the wall-stumps lay a bed of blue clay upon which the walls of the existing house 5 and the retaining wall of the surrounding midden platform rested.

In the grass slope between this early house and passage A is a hatch. This gives access to a sewer, the walls of which are 76 cm to 107 cm high. The channel seems to have run eastward from beneath passage B; it was traced under the west wall of house 5 and found to open into a ruinous oval chamber beneath the floor. The chamber may have been a cistern or a sump. It had collapsed and been filled in before house 5 was built.

A huge block of midden sloping south-east once extended from the back of houses 4 and

5 to the south-east corner of house 7. A large slice of this has been removed, exposing two houses of period 1, numbered respectively 9 and 10. Over house 9 no less than seven distinct layers of midden, each separated by thin streaks of sand, could be distinguished. Five of these layers surround the retaining wall of house 5 but the wall itself rests on a sixth layer of midden that runs over the wall-stumps of house 9.

House 9 is the best-preserved structure of period 1. It possesses the usual central hearth, a pillared dresser against the rear south-east wall, and a beehive cell in the south corner. One check of the door may still be discerned, with the bar-hole intact, but most of the front wall had been disturbed when the cell opening off passage C was built. The beds are not built out from the side walls but take the form of wide alcoves set into the thickness of the walls on either side of the hearth. They are partitioned off from the rest of the chamber in the normal way by large slabs on edge. The back wall of the south-west bed-alcove is preserved to a sufficient height to show a marked inward corbelling especially at the corners. This alcove was in fact a corbelled apse. The recessing of the beds into the walls as opposed to the free-standing beds of period 2 is the only significant feature in the internal design of the houses that changes in the two periods. The preservation of the right-hand

House 9. This is one of the earliest houses in the village: note that the beds (to the left and right) are recessed into the thickness of the wall rather than projecting into the living area as in the later houses.

wall is due to its incorporation in the wall of passage C, which remained in use throughout period 2. On the floor of the house were found potsherds and bone tools, similar to those from later dwellings, and a piece of deer's antler perforated and hollowed out at one end to serve as the mount of a stone adze-head.

House 10 is almost completely ruined, only just enough surviving of the walls to make the general outline distinguishable. A cell in one corner and two of the three uprights of a dresser may also be recognised. Two stone axe-heads, some broken bone pins and several smashed pots, most richly decorated, lay on the floor. This was covered with sand, partly overlaid with a greenish deposit that seems to represent the discharge from a drain, perhaps from an early version of the drain from house 5. Upon this discharge rested a very broken pavement which ran over the stumps of the house walls. The wall supporting the platform round house 4 rested on this pavement. The stone box, shaped like a normal hearth, but paved with a stone slab and unmarked by fire, to the east of the hut, may belong to the same period as the paving. Its use is unknown.

Finally, **house 4'** lies under and to the east of house 4. Indeed the east wall of the latter runs across the floor of the older structure. Hence only a segment of the latter is visible, and to expose even this it was necessary to remove a section of the wall supporting the platform round house 4 (the latter was in any case in a bad state of preservation). It was entered from the east. All that survives are the right-hand check of the door, with the facing-slab perforated for the bar-hole, a beehive cell on the right of the door (partially blocked by a secondary buttress), and a recess, divided into two compartments (one now filled), that was perhaps a dresser. A curious artificial pit-mark will be noticed in the end of the top slab of the dresser's central pier.

The wall to the left of the doorway had been pulled down when house 4 was built. At the same time a hole was broken through the cell for the drain which flows across under the floor of house 4.

The door of house 4' gives on to a stamped earth floor, 15 cm above the house floor and belonging to a sort of passage or alley. In front of the door the foundations of a curving wall, rectilinear on the seaward side, can just be made out. This construction may have been a porch, similar to that built on to structure 8 and designed, like that, to shelter the door from the wind. Such porches would have been necessary in period 1 because insufficient midden would have been accumulated to provide protection from the wind, and the structures would have been largely free-standing. Across the porch's wall-stumps runs a section of a later drainage channel, very neatly constructed. The 'passage' through this porch led downward on to an open paved area, now covered with turf, sloping away to the south-east. The pavement, like that of the Market Place to the west, rests on an artificially laid blue-clay bedding. Under this clay were found the ruins of a wall and a midden deposit nearly 91 cm deep, which must belong to the earliest phase of period 1 in the history of the village.

A small number of implements of stone and bone, beads, and examples of pottery discovered during the excavations are exhibited at the monument. The major collection of relics is to be seen in the National Museum of Antiquities of Scotland, Edinburgh, but representative selections have been deposited in the local museums at Kirkwall and Stromness, and in the British Museum.

Printed in Scotland for HMSO c.c. 18023 Dd. 287273 C52 1/89 H.F. 4103